AF483085

This book belongs to

____

Grandmama Loves you Max and Emma.

Copyright © 2024

Cecilia D Porter

All rights reserved.

GOD MADE ME!

Cecilia D. Porter

God you made me to be exactly
what He wanted me to be.

God made me and gave me a heart.

I can feel my heart beating.

God made me and gave me my eyes.
I can see all the beautiful things
He made.

God made me and gave me a face.
I am beautiful just the way I am.

God made me and gave me legs.

I can walk and run.

God made and me and gave me a brain.

I can think all by myself.

God made me and gave me hair.
My hair is perfectly for me.

God made me and gave me hair.
My hair is perfectly for me.

God made me and gave me a mouth to speak. Listen as I praise His holy name.

God made me special
from head to toe.

God made me just to be me.

"I praise you because I am fearfully
and wonderfully made; your works are wonderful..."
(Psalm 139:14)